BBC

1960   2010

TELEVISION CENTRE

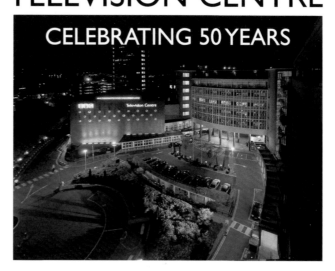

CELEBRATING 50 YEARS

OF GREAT BROADCASTING

GRAND DESIGNS - building Television Centre

UP AND RUNNING - first night nerves

FULL SWING - the 1960s

GLITTERING STARS - the 1970s

BROADCAST NEWS - the 1980s

SUIT YOU SIR - the 1990s

STRICTLY BRITAIN - the 2000s

Design and editorial by Nick McCann
Decade introductions by Robert Seatter, Head of BBC History
Produced and published for the BBC by Heritage House Group

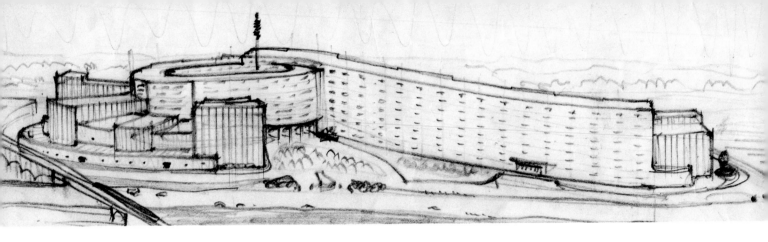

IT ALL BEGAN WITH A QUESTION:

December 1949: when asked to come up with an architectural concept for the first ever purpose-built TV building in the world, architect Graham Dawbarn doodled a question mark on the back of an envelope... then realised he had by accident found the perfect shape for Television Centre!

Here is his original doodle (left), plus an architect's drawing and scale model of the site.

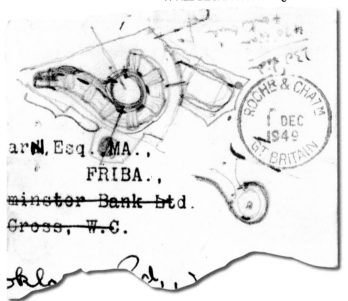

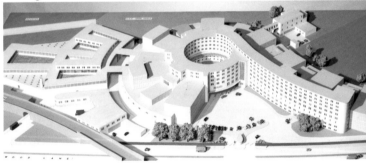

Television centre in the early days with the vast Studio 1 - at over 10,000 sq metres - to the left.

1950s: BBC Television Centre transforms the White City area and becomes one of the centres of world television

ELEGANT CURVES:
1956: 'Leslie Roberts Silhouettes', a popular variety act of the time, appeared on the Billy Cotton Band Show, and are seen here in a publicity shot adjacent to the curvaceous girders of the Television Centre rotunda.

GRAND DESIGNS

Often affectionately called "the doughnut" by members of staff, – famously, Sir Terry Wogan – the building was begun in 1951, with the foundation stone bearing the date 1956. The complete question mark shape took some years to complete. It was not until 1996, with the addition of the News Centre that the question mark received its final dot (the circular lift shaft viewed from above). Other buildings were added over the years, but the essential design and shape of Television Centre remains the same.

1959:
Artist John Piper was commissioned to create a wonderful, colourful mosaic for the building's reception. It remains in situ today. Piper also famously created the great stained glass window of Coventry Cathedral after its destruction in WWII.

The statue of the sun god, 'Helios', by T.B. Huxley Jones, in the centre of the main block (right), was created to evoke the power of television, with the two figures underneath symbolising 'sound' and 'vision'. The fountain at its base was only a limited success, however. The sound of tinkling water made all the employees run to the toilet, so it was quickly turned off!

UP AND RUNNING...

So in 1960, Television Centre opened, an airy and hyper-modern building of its time, described by the then Director of Television as 'a factory capable of producing about 1,500 hours a year of black and white programmes'. It featured brand new TV technology and functional but stylish design – here's the staff canteen (soon to be the butt of every performer's joke about its terrible tea and coffee) and below it, the main reception with its distinctive curved shape, where stars would mingle with staff and members of the general public.

THEN & NOW:
50 years ago when it began its life, Television Centre had seven studios, made only black and white TV programmes and produced no news at all. But it was THE place to be - at the cutting edge of television innovation. Nowhere else like it!

Programme-making continued in parallel at other televison studios in the location, such as the BBC's Lime Grove Studios, but gradually over time Television Centre became the focus for all major activity.

Now, it is the iconic home of British television - a Grade II listed building, with 11 fully-equipped digital widescreen studios and top-notch news facilities - three studios, six radio stations, 12 radio workshop studios and 25 TV edit suites. Oh, and possibly the most famous children's garden in the UK (Blue Peter, of course). Over 5,000 staff work here, and 240 million viewers around the world watch BBC News programmes made in this building.

The producer and his immediate production team sit anxiously studying the studio floor on the first night of broadcasting from Television Centre. In many ways the operation of a studio has changed little, with the same basic formula and principles working today, plus anxiety, stress and potential tantrums...!

The First Night Show is a packed variety show, and the Radio Times cover of the week features three of its most popular stars: magician David Nixon, children's entertainer 'Mr Pastry' and the enduringly popular Arthur Askey. Also on the bill are dance and music from The Irving Davies Dancers, The George Mitchell Singers and The Television Toppers.

26 June 1960: BBC Television's first night , with live orchestra and all those first night nerves.

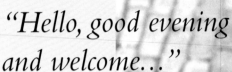

"Hello, good evening and welcome…"

DAVID FROST, host of the ground-breaking That Was The Week That Was, went on to become one of the most recognisable faces of the BBC and broadcasting across the world for over 40 years.

He is the only person to have interviewed all British Prime Ministers between 1964 and 2009. His interview of disgraced American President, Richard Nixon became the stuff of legend, most recently portrayed by Michael Sheen in the Ron Howard movie. He received an OBE in 1970 and was knighted in 1993.

That Was The Week That Was

FULL SWING - the 1960s

A host of popular comedians, entertainers, singers and dancers features on *The First Night Show*. Acts such as these are to figure throughout the decade, one of the most popular being *The Black and White Minstrels* (watched at its peak by 18 million viewers).

From 1964, it runs alongside a new music phenomenon, *Top of the Pops* – who can forget the star appearances of The Beatles, Dusty Springfield, The Rolling Stones and so many more; its team of curvaceous professional dancers called Pan's People; and most of all its gyrating studio audience?!

But it was the decade of drama greats too – *The Wednesday Play/Play for Today* bring contemporary issues searingly onto the small screen. *The Forsyte Saga* (the last drama serial recorded in black and white, 1967) is so popular that it stops social life and even changes the timing of church services, while later that same year *Vanity Fair* portrays classic drama in colour for the first time ever. And *Dr Finlay's Casebook*, *Z Cars* and *Softly, Softly* reinvent medical and police drama respectively. BBC Comedy has a run of huge hits in the 60s – remember *Steptoe & Son*, *Dad's Army*, *The Dick Emery Show*, *The Likely Lads* and of course the fantastically popular *Morecambe & Wise*?

But comedy shocks too. Broadcast campaigner Mary Whitehouse decries *Till Death us Do Part* as a moral outrage. *That Was The Week That Was*, the first real late night satire show, causes consternation in Parliament, but makes a star of its presenter, David Frost. While right at the end of the decade, *Monty Python's Flying Circus* transforms TV comedy all over again – 'And now for something completely different!'

And of course this is the time of technological innovation and expansion, not always without difficulty! Memorably, a second channel, BBC2 launches in 1964, introducing better screen definition (625 lines replacing the earlier uniquely British system of 405 lines). However, the channel is prevented from broadcasting its opening night because of a power failure in London. But the journey continues, and all through the 60s, *Tomorrow's World* brings science's newest inventions right into our living room, while Patrick Moore shows us all how to look at *The Sky at Night*.

Finally, the BBC News operation moves into Television Centre (from its earlier home in Alexandra Palace) at the very end of this decade, and so puts news firmly at the heart of the building's very busy whirl of broadcast activity.

Blue Peter

Arguably the most iconic trio of all: Valerie Singleton, Peter Purves and John Noakes. Every child in the land just HAD to own a Blue Peter Badge.

"Here's one we made earlier"

It happened here...
The desecration of the Blue Peter Garden 1978

Nearing completion, the Blue Peter Italian sunken garden was partially vandalised in April 1978. Causing a lot of distress to resident gardener Percy Thrower (opposite page, top row, centre), presenters and viewers, the damage was repaired. Worse was to come just five years later when oil was poured into the water and the sun dial was smashed. The culprits were never found, although the last series of *Ashes to Ashes* (BBC One), would have us believe that it was Gene Hunt...!

1 1968: Peter, Valerie and John, with the original pets.

2 1968: Peter, Lesley Judd and John, with cats and legendary Shep.

3 1973: John's record-breaking free-fall with the Red Devils.

4 1974: the famous 'makes': Lesley's valentine for John.

5 1980: Percy Thrower and Sarah Greene in the Garden.

6 1982: Simon Groom, Peter Duncan with boomerangs at Television Centre.

7 1998: Konnie, Stuart and Katy raise money for Mozambique.

8 1999: Konnie in the Garden with the new sculpture.

9 2000: new and original presenters open the 1971 time capsule.

10 2010: Joel Defries, Helen Skelton, Andy Akinwolere and Lucy.

"How's about that then?"

Launched in 1964 from a converted church hall in Manchester by its very first presenter Jimmy Savile, Top of the Pops went on to be a huge hit at Television Centre (when the programme switched to colour in late 1969). And remarkably, some of the bands and artists are still going, notably The Rolling Stones and Cliff Richard.

The show was originally scheduled to run for only a few programmes. It actually ran for over 42 years, many of those programmes recorded at Television Centre.

1	I WANT TO HOLD YOUR HAND The Beatles
2	GLAD ALL OVER The Dave Clark Five
3	SHE LOVES YOU The Beatles
4	YOU WERE MADE FOR ME Freddie & The Dreamers
5	I ONLY WANT TO BE WITH YOU Dusty Springfield
6	24 HOURS FROM TULSA Gene Pitney
7	DOMINIQUE The Singing Nun
8	SECRET LOVE Kathy Kirby
9	SWINGIN' ON A STAR Big Dee Irwin
10	HIPPY HIPPY SHAKE Swinging Blue Jeans
11	MARIA ELENA Los Indios Tabajaras
12	DON'T TALK TO HIM Cliff Richard
13	I WANNA BE YOUR MAN The Rolling Stones
14	THE BEATLES (L.P.) The Beatles
15	...e Shadows
	... (E.P.) The Beatles
	Elvis Presley
	...LK ALONE Ger...
	Chris Sandf...
	E.P.) The...

Top of the Pops

Dusty Springfield charms the TOTP audience while the show's host, Pete Murray, has a brief rest from the camera.

The Eurovision Song Contest 1963

Eurovision Song Contest Director, Yvonne Littlewood, on the roof of Television Centre with the helicopter used for the 1963 show.

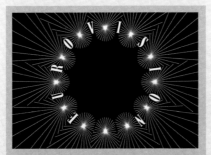

It happened here...
Circled by helicopter in the opening titles, Television Centre was the setting for the 1963 Eurovision Song Contest. Just three years old, the Centre was promoted as Europe's most advanced production facility. Presenter Katie Boyle (right), the scoreboard, and the audience, were housed in one studio; performers and orchestra occupied the other.

"This is London calling"

Dramatic Licence

The Wednesday Play

ON CAMERA:
Harold Pinter stars in his production of The Wednesday Play *in 1964, 'In Camera'.*

Like his fellow playwright John Osborne, Pinter acted as well as wrote and directed.

These short dramas set the standard for much of what came later: gritty, social stories tackling 'real life'.

1962-1978: Z Cars created a completely new type of TV crime drama. In contrast to the safe and cosy world of Dixon of Dock Green, starring the avuncular Jack Warner - signing off each episode with "Evening All" - its stars Stratford Johns and Frank Windsor were involved in a much grittier and more realistic portrayal of police work. Remarkably, the original series was one of the last British TV dramas which was regularly screened live, providing a greater sense of pace and immediacy.

'Horror of Darkness' - Glenda Jackson as 'Cathy' in another Wednesday Play, written by John Hopkins and directed by Anthony Page.

This powerful and courageous piece held the audience for a full 90 minutes and was broadcast in March 1965. Glenda Jackson went on to a fabulous career on stage, screen, and perhaps most notably, Morecambe & Wise! She then changed direction totally and entered politics.

GREAT FORESIGHT: The Forsyte Saga by John Galsworthy, became one of the most successful dramas in television history. Here the stars line up on the set, among them: Eric Porter as a fiercely patriarchal 'Soames', Susan Hampshire as 'Fleur', Nyree Dawn Porter as 'Irene' and a youthful-looking Martin Jarvis (fourth from left) as 'Jon'.

"VANITY, VANITY, ALL IS VANITY":
Vanity Fair: Susan Hampshire is bursting with joy, viewing her Regency outfits for this colourful period drama.

1967 was Susan Hampshire's year: she creates the groundbreaking role of 'Fleur' in The Forsyte Saga, then goes on to play 'Becky Sharp' in Vanity Fair (see left), the first BBC period drama made in colour.

The Dick Emery Show

A man of many faces, seen here outside Television Centre with some of his on-screen team including the ever popular Joan Sims and Una Stubbs.

But he could transform himself into...

"Oooh you are awful..."

"...but I like you"

The searing, controversial and hysterical Till Death Us Do Part, starred Warren Mitchell as Alf Garnett. Dandy Nicholls played his resigned and long-suffering wife ("The Silly Moo") and Una Stubbs and Anthony Booth ("The Scouse Git"), supported as daughter and shiftless son-in-law. In real life, Booth's daughter, Cherie, became Tony Blair's wife.

"That's charming that is..."

"You Silly Moo!"

'You're bleedin' mad you are Dad"

"What are you talking about Dad?!"

1964: NOT ONLY BUT ALSO, *was very nearly just 'not only', being originally devised as a platform for the multi-talented musician, pianist and comedian, Dudley Moore and his guests. Being unsure about going it alone he asked his* Beyond the Fringe *partner and collaborator Peter Cook to guest on the first show with Diahann Carroll and Beatle John Lennon. The success of their double-act, especially Moore's constant corpsing in 'The Dagenham Dialogues', led to Cook becoming a permanent fixture, and the rest as they say, is history. Cruelly, the brilliant Moore died of a rare, degenerative brain disorder.*

Not Only

"Goodbyeee"

But Also

1965: Peter Cook and Dudley Moore, not only larking about, but also creating a new form in comedy - 'alternative'   15

Steptoe & Son

"You dirty old man"

Harry H. Corbett and Wilfrid Brambell
in the dark, claustrophobic, sad, funny and unique
Steptoe & Son written by Galton & Simpson.
The BBC made eight series beginning in 1962,
ending in 1974. There were also Christmas Specials
and feature films. Series One to Four were made in
black and white, and the remaining four series in colour.

Dad's Army

"*You stupid boy!*"

Bringing sunshine

Dad's Army *and* Morecambe & Wise *brought much laughter to our screens during the decade. Catch-phrases such as Arthur Lowe's "You stupid boy!" and Eric's "What do you think of it so far?", became part of everyday vocabulary. Dad's Army and Morecambe & Wise were arguably two of the most universally loved shows on British television, and remain so to many people world-wide today.*

A youthful Eric and Ernie outside a sunlit Television Centre.

That Was
The Week
That Was

David Frost, with Roy Kinnear, Kenneth Cope, Lance Percival and Willie Rushton looking studious on the panel of the first real satirical show on television, 'TW3', as it was affectionately known. Ned Sherrin produced.

The glamour was provided by singer, actress and comedienne Millicent (Millie) Martin, who closed the show each week with a belting rendition of the theme song, "That Was The Week That Was!"

Unsparing in its lampooning of politicians and other establishment figures, the show coincided with the Profumo affair and the politician along with many others became the subject of the panel's derision.

'Millie Martin' in her trademark little black dress and perched on her trademark high stool, sang the show out. 'TW3' was unusual in televisual terms in exposing all the technical workings of its studio activity, cameras, cables etc...

"And now for something completely different"

Monty Python's Flying Circus

1969: The Pythons, (back row) Graham Chapman (with the pipe), Eric Idle, Terry Gilliam (front row) Terry Jones, John Cleese and Michael Palin created the anarchic comedy, Monty Python's Flying Circus. 45 episodes were made over four series, and later, several hugely successful films, stage performances and shows. Graham Chapman died in 1989.

THE MORNING OF LIFE:
Before the formation of 'The Pythons' proper, Cleese, Chapman, Jones, Idle and Palin honed their craft in the 'Footlights Revue' at Cambridge University. It was later that genius American animator, Terry Gilliam, joined, and added the surreal animations to the show which gave it its unique visual style.

'Pythonesque' - a new word for outrageous and absurdist comedy - entered the English dictionary. Comedy was never the same again!

"Stop that it's silly"

'They think it's all over...'

LOOK AND LISTEN
Radio Tim
BBC tv and radio

ENGLAND 4

Left to right:
Captain Bobby Moore, scorer
of the final goal Geoff Hurst,
Martin Peters and goalkeeper
Gordon Banks. On the Wembley
Stadium gantry (above), an
advertisement for the
Radio Times.

Radio Times
WORLD CUP NUMBER

It was a baking hot day in July 1966, when BBC Sport
commentator Kenneth Wolstenholme uttered the now
immortal lines: 'They think it's all over... It is now', and
England had won the World Cup. Years later, in 1995,
BBC launched its popular sports quiz, titling it with
those same famous words.

'...It is now!'

Photo: Evening Standard / Hulton Archive / Getty Images

The 1966 World Cup was an iconic sporting moment, the first major event to be hosted and co-ordinated from studios at Television Centre. It was also innovative technologically, featuring the first ever use of 'action replay' and 'slow motion'. Further innovations from the Centre were to follow: first major sporting event in colour was Wimbledon in 1967; first Olympic Games in colour was the Munich Games of 1972; even the very first breakfast TV show, which was Breakfast with Brisbane in 1982, tying in to Commonwealth Games of the same year, and so on…

The Centre was also of course famous for its regular flagship sports programming. From the late 1960s /early 70s onwards, Sportsnight, Grandstand and Match of the Day were all done live from these studios, making household names of their presenters, David Coleman, Harry Carpenter, Jimmy Hill, Des Lynam, Frank Bough etc, and creating huge audiences at regular points in the watching week.

Today, Television Centre is the engine room that brings great sport action and results to audiences wherever they are, working across television, radio and online. Its website is the most popular sport website in the UK.

The 1966 World Cup BBC Sports commentator team in the Television Centre rotunda.

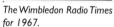
The Wimbledon Radio Times for 1967.

Jimmy Hill: the face of Match of the Day during the 1970s / 80s.

Grandstand with David Coleman.

A Question of Sport with David Coleman (centre), Ian Botham (left) and Bill Beaumont.

Some of the regulars on They Think It's All Over.

Today's Match of the Day presented by Gary Lineker.

BBC SPORTS PERSONALITY OF THE YEAR

Devised in 1954, the BBC Sports Personality of the Year soon became a regular feature in the Television Centre calendar. So many talented and popular sportsmen and women have stepped up to receive the coveted television camera trophy. One of the most moving was Muhammad Ali (Cassius Clay as was), who battled against severe illness to take the Sports Personality of the Century award in 1999 (above).

The 2009 winner was footballer Ryan Giggs.

On top of the world! - the summer of '69

... or on top of the roof of Television Centre, to be precise. Exuberant dance troupe Pan's People, choreographed by Flick Colby (third left), became a permanent fixture on Top of the Pops, with their energetic routines causing a sensation.

Top of the Pops

The Age of Aquarius continued with the momentous landing on the Moon during the summer of '69, watched by millions of people across the globe. BBC Science Correspondent, James Burke, was in his element and became the face and voice of The Space Age.

Andi!   Louise!   Flick!

Patrick Moore's The Sky at Night *has had an enduring appeal for audiences. Beginning in 1957, this programme remains one of the longest running on television, in the UK, the world, and the universe!*

Ruth!

Babs!

Dee Dee!

24   Shirley Bassey's 'spectaculars' prove hugely popular and characterise a new glamour in light entertainment

GLITTERING STARS - the 1970s

olour TV, launched at the end of the 1960s, really comes into its own in this decade. It reinvents the historical costume drama – remember the opulent costumes and dramatic storylines of *The Six Wives of Henry VIII* or *Elizabeth R* (starring Oscar-winning actress Glenda Jackson)? Glenda recalls that it took at least six hours to apply her makeup for the later episodes. And Derek Jacobi, the star of *I, Claudius*, has a similarly labour-intensive time peeling off the layers of his elderly Roman tyrant… It's the decade also that Television Centre begins the dramatisation of all 37 of Shakespeare's plays – from 1978 onwards.

Once again, BBC Comedy gives us so many memorable moments, from John Cleese's eccentric hotelier in *Fawlty Towers* berating his long-suffering wife and incompetent waiter Manuel, to the first eco-comedy, as Richard Briers and Felicity Kendal grapple with self-sufficiency in Surbiton (*The Good Life*); from Frankie Howerd's never-ending attempt to complete his opening prologue (*Up Pompeii!*) to the familiar sign-off of *The Two Ronnies* ('So it's goodnight from me. And it's goodnight from him'). And not forgetting the retail innuendo of *Are You Being Served?*: 'I'm free!' Finally, *Morecambe & Wise* 'Christmas Specials' become family institutions in this decade, and their 1977 show is watched by an incredible 28 million viewers! One of the duo's star guests, among many, is Shirley Bassey, who has a run of phenomenally successful 'spectaculars' in the 1970s, all coming out of Television Centre and featuring a cast of glittering guests.

On a more intimate note, Michael Parkinson interviews the roll call of the famous and the infamous (who could forget Muhammad Ali, Richard Burton, Orson Welles, the list goes on…?), while Children's TV creates some of its most popular series. *Playschool* invites younger viewers every morning to explore life through the round, square or arched window; *Blue Peter* continues to engage children with its charity campaigns, its journeys around the world, and its famous 'makes' ('Here's one I made earlier'); and *Grange Hill* gives an unforgettable take on life in the British classroom. *Jim'll Fix It* sees Jimmy Savile making children's dreams come true.

Last but not least, in this decade the Time Lord (Jon Pertwee the third Doctor) moves to Television Centre recording nearly all his studio scenes inside the building. Previous Doctors had time-travelled to and from a variety of external BBC studios, though post colour TV, the series is always recorded here, up to 1989. In total, seven Doctors record at Television Centre.

John Hurt as Caligula in the BBC adaptation of I, Claudius

Derek Jacobi scrubs down after filming I, Claudius

Siân Phillips as Livia in I, Claudius

Glenda Jackson in the title role in Elizabeth R (three pictures). The makeup took literally hours to apply

Anthony Hopkins in BBC Shakespeare's Othello

Bob Hoskins in BBC Shakespeare's Othello

Michael Hordern in BBC Shakespeare's King Lear

The 1970s at Television Centre are a magnet for stars of stage and screen, lending their talents to the best of British drama

Cheryl Campbell in Testament of Youth

Zoe Wanamaker in BBC Shakespeare's Richard III

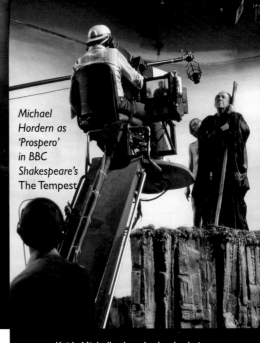
Michael Hordern as 'Prospero' in BBC Shakespeare's The Tempest

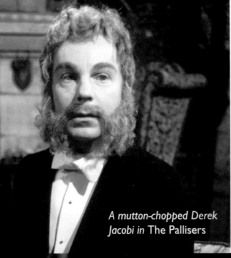
A mutton-chopped Derek Jacobi in The Pallisers

'All the world's a stage…

The many faces of BBC drama

…and all the men and women merely players'

Keith Michell takes the lead role in The Six Wives of Henry VIII

John Thaw in BBC Shakespeare's King John

Jonathan Miller directing Antony and Cleopatra

Bob Hoskins and Cheryl Campbell in Dennis Potter's Pennies from Heaven

"Yes my little nest of vipers"

"Que?"

"Basil!"

"A satisfied customer...
we should have 'em stuffed"

Fawlty Towers aka Watery Fowls
Flay Otters
Fatty Owls
Farty Towels

PURE GENIUS:
Fawlty Towers was inspired by The Gleneagles Hotel in Torquay, and particularly by its manager whom John Cleese ('Basil Fawlty'), described as 'the most marvellously rude man I've ever met'. The two series (remarkably only 12 programmes were made), became comic classics and are always in the top ten of anything funny. Prunella Scales played Basil's wife 'Sybil' and the much-abused Spanish waiter 'Manuel' was deftly portrayed by Andrew Sachs. Interiors were recorded at Television Centre, while outside scenes were shot on film on location. The opening credits were accompanied by a shot of the hotel sign in varying states of disrepair, and in the second series, they developed into increasingly surreal and naughty anagrams (see above).

The 1970s is a golden age of comedy writing. *Fawlty Towers*, written by husband and wife team John Cleese and Connie Booth, is a huge hit

Last of the Summer Wine
by Roy Clarke. CAST: Bill Owen, Peter Sallis, Kathy Staff and many others.

It Ain't Half Hot Mum
by Jimmy Perry and David Croft. CAST: Windsor Davies, Melvyn Hayes, Don Estelle and others.

The Good Life
by John Esmonde and Bob Larbey. CAST: Richard Briers, Felicity Kendal, Penelope Keith, Paul Eddington.

(and HM The Queen visits!)

Porridge
by Dick Clement and Ian Le Frenais. CAST: Ronnie Barker, Richard Beckinsale, Fulton Mackay and many others.

"Naff off!"

CLASSICS ALL:
The fondness in which these situation comedies were, and still are held, is testament to the writing, the acting and the warmth of the pieces in general. Each series was packed with lovable characters, unforgettable moments and abundant catch-phrases.

But **ALL** 30 series of the elderly rural romp, *Last of the Summer Wine*, are written by one man, Roy Clarke

Up Pompeii! *starred Frankie Howerd as the slave, Lurcio, whose constant reprimand to the TV audience was "Oh well, please yourself."*

'Ada Shufflebotham' and 'Cissie Braithwaite', aka Les Dawson (left) and Roy Barraclough (right), a routine from The Les Dawson Show.

"THE POUND IN YOUR POCKET":
PM Harold Wilson, along with Michael Crawford's 'Frank Spencer', were among the public's favourite characters by the first truly superstar impressionist, Mike Yarwood, recorded at Television Centre and other nearby venues.

ONE OF THE ALL TIME GREATS: Eric Sykes CBE, is both performer and writer. After co-writing The Goon Show *among many other things, he went on to appear in his own show,* Sykes *with on-screen sister, Hattie Jacques.*

Are You Being Served? *starred John Inman (left), Mollie Sugden, Wendy Richards, Frank Thornton, Trevor Bannister and Nicholas Smith. Department stores were viewed in a whole new light...*

The Two Ronnies' *hilarious take on the musical 'Grease' (left). On location filming (right): Barker is 'Piggy Malone' and Corbett is 'Charlie Farlie', in one of their mystery serials, the most famous being 'The Phantom Raspberry Blower of Old London Town', 1976, written by Spike Milligan.*

The Two Ronnies (Corbett and Barker)

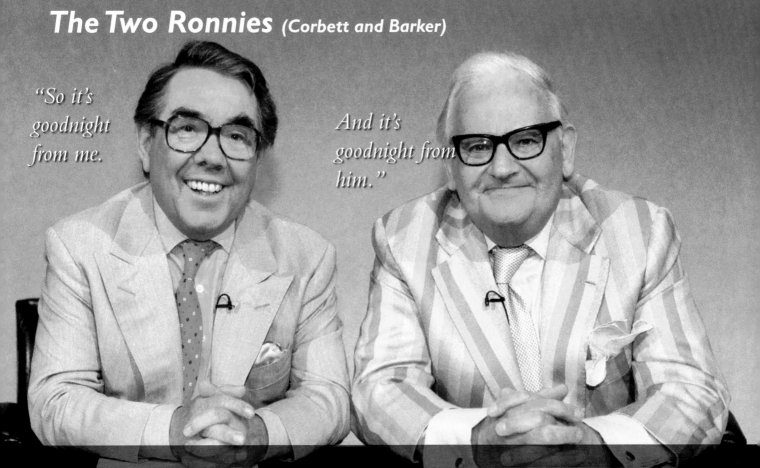

"So it's goodnight from me.

And it's goodnight from him."

1974: The Cliff Richard Show -
*The Three Degrees and the first ever
TV appearance of the Nolans,
all acts singing together.*

1975: *Johnny Mathis with Lulu.*

1970: *Cilla in her own show.
Many of the above were recorded at
The Television Theatre, nearby to
Television Centre.*

Morecambe & Wise (and Cliff Richard)

*Their early career in the music halls of the North
gave Eric and Ernie a love of song and dance.
Their impeccable timing and talent - Ernie for one was
a superb hoofer - gave the star-studded comic numbers
a polish and sophistication over and above the gags
and slapstick. The production values, the lavish sets in
Television Centre's largest studio, and the costumes and
musical arrangements were second to none.*

*"What do you
think of it so far?"*

'Gotta sing - gotta dance'

A song ends every *Morecambe & Wise* show - the most memorable perhaps being 'Bring Me Sunshine'

"I am playing all the right notes.
Just not necessarily in the right order."

"Rubbish!"

Conductor and pianist, André Previn ('Andrew Preview'), in the
all-time classic sketch where Eric tries to play a concerto.

Glenda Jackson in one of Ernie's plays 'wot he rote'.

It happened here... All Star Record Breakers 1977

The late, great, and
multi-talented Roy Castle.

Stars from BBC Television
tap danced their way around
the circular 'doughnut' area of
Television Centre, setting a new
world record for the largest mass
tap dance in history. *Roy Castle's
All Star Record Breakers* dominated
the schedules between Christmas
and New Year 1977.

Besty, the original 'Gorgeous George': football's George Best.

Charm personified: David Niven.

Imagine: troubled genius, John Lennon.

Hollywood legend: 'Gentleman Jim', James Stewart.

Beauty and The Beast: you guess...

'Putting on the Ritz': Fred Astaire.

Billy, 'The Big Yin', Connolly.

Carrying on at the 'Queen Vic': Barbara Windsor.

The 'Absolutely Fabulous' Joanna Lumley.

'The Greatest' of them all: Muhammad Ali, formerly Cassius Clay.

Australia's 'First Lady': Dame Edna Everage, aka Barry Humphries.

The glamorous Joan Collins.

When he interviewed Rod Hull in 1976, the comedian's glove puppet Emu suddenly attacked Parky, drawing blood and causing him to fall off his chair. Despite all of the famous personalities he had interviewed, he feared he'd always be remembered for -

"That bloody bird"

Now of course **Sir** Michael Parkinson, he began as a journalist on regional newspapers, then television in his native Yorkshire. His Saturday night show became total stay-at-home viewing, with a regular procession of Hollywood legends, sports stars, statesmen, and the great and the good from both sides of the Atlantic. The resident band, the Harry Stoneham orchestra, accompanied top class singers and musicians. An enthusiastic jazz fan, Michael Parkinson was responsible for championing many up and coming singers and musicians, Diana Krall and Jamie Cullum among many others.

Photo: Terry O'Neill / Getty Images

BBC Weather has evolved hugely over the last half century, from a handful of weathermen using very basic graphics to a large team of about 25 presenters interpreting ever more sophisticated virtual visuals. All the BBC weather presenters are actually employees of the Meteorological Office and most have formal forecasting qualifications.

1963-1974: Bert Foord, one of the first weathermen at Television Centre to become a household name.

Midday tomorrow

LOW

HIGH

"*Turned out nice again*"

The Weather

1975-2000: Bill Giles went on to present the weather for 25 years.

1969-1983: Jack Scott was the first to introduce the magnetic weather symbols.

TONIGHT

Magnetic rubbers to computer-generated graphics: how we present the weather changes dramatically every decade

Gales, freezing temperatures and snow - a typical British summer!

Michael Fish's infamous weather forecast of October 1987, in which he scotched rumours of a hurricane across the UK, has gone down in broadcasting history. There's just one problem - he claims he never said those fatal words!

1993-2005: Helen Young (below), the youngest weather presenter when she began the job at 24.

Top: Barbara Edwards, 1975

Middle: Ian McCaskill, 1979

Above: John Kettley, 1993

"And don't worry there's not going to be a hurricane."

Robert Dougall

Peter Woods

Angela Rippon

Richard Baker

Richard Whitmore

John Humphrys and John Simpson

Moira Stuart

Good News

Sue Lawley

Michael Buerk

Peter Sissons

George Alagiah and Sophie Raworth

Huw Edwards

"Here is the BBC News"

Some of the faces of BBC News: the largest news service in the world. BBC News becomes increasingly engaged with making election

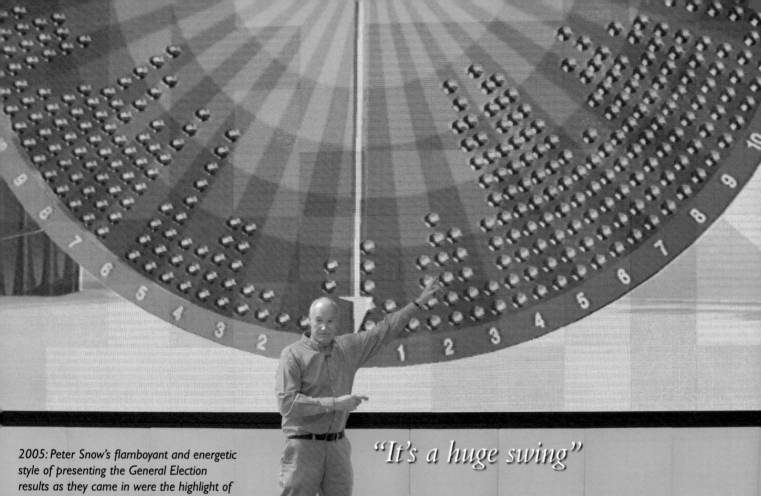

2005: Peter Snow's flamboyant and energetic style of presenting the General Election results as they came in were the highlight of the evening's viewing. The 'swingometer', used to demonstrate how the voting was affecting the parties' gains and losses, became more elaborate with each election.

"It's a huge swing"

Vote of confidence

nights clear for audiences - from the innovative 1950s Swingometer to Jeremy Vine's 2010 'virtual stairway' to 10 Downing Street

David Dimbleby, son of the famous broadcaster Richard Dimblebly whose news report from Belsen concentration camp moved many to tears, has been a longstanding BBC commentator and presenter of countless current affairs programmes. He was also the anchorman for the 2010 election night, staying up some 18 hours to see the results to their uncertain conclusion.

The 2010 Election Studio.

BLUFF 3

The delightfully engaging Call My Bluff, fronted by Robert Robinson.

One of the very first celebrity chefs, 'Dame Delia' Smith.

The Old Grey Whistle Test with 'Whispering' Bob Harris. Nice...

OLD GREY WHISTLE TEST

The Generation Game with Bruce Forsyth and Anthea Redfern.

That's Life with Esther Rantzen and the chocolate-voiced Cyril Fletcher and team.

Doctor Who is one of the most popular TV shows ever devised by the BBC. Generations of children have grown up with their version of the Doctor - be it the original, ex-Shakespearean actor Wiliam Hartnell, the be-scarfed Tom Baker, or the much later, tongue-in-cheek hero, David Tennant.

From the opening notes of its distinctive theme tune (devised by Delia Derbyshire of the BBC Radiophonic Workshop after a composition by Ron Grainer), many children would be heading straight for a hiding place behind the sofa - at the prospect of the arrival of Cybermen, Autons, Yeti, Sensorites, and worst of all, the invincible Daleks.

The show was recorded at a number of different studios, not exclusively Television Centre - the first episode to be recorded there was in 1964, the last in 1989; the third Doctor, Jon Pertwee (1970-74), recorded nearly all his studio scenes at the Centre. All of the following Doctors have, at one time or another, landed their Tardis here: William Hartnell, Patrick Troughton, Jon Pertwee, Tom Baker, Peter Davison, Colin Baker, Sylvester McCoy. Since its latest reinvention in 2005, Doctor Who has been based in Cardiff, produced by BBC Cymru Wales.

"Exterminate, exterminate!!!"

Doctor Who

IS THERE A DOCTOR IN THE HOUSE?!

Clockwise from top left: William Hartnell, Patrick Troughton & Jon Pertwee, Peter Davison, Sylvester McCoy, Colin Baker and Tom Baker.

The Tardis, which appears from the outside to be a 1950s police box, is actually an acronym for 'Time And Relative Dimension In Space' 43

BROADCAST NEWS - the 1980s

This is a challenging decade, with war and turbulence around the world: BBC News correspondents send in reports to Television Centre from the Falklands War, and from dangerous events in Tiananmen Square, the Soviet Union, Eastern Europe and Northern Ireland, as well as from the Miners' strike nearer home. In Ethiopia, Michael Buerk alerts the world to a famine of biblical proportions, leading to Bob Geldof's *Live Aid* phenomenon in 1985 which raises more than £60 million for Famine Relief Foundation.

It's also the wedding of the century, when Lady Diana Spencer marries Prince Charles (1981), watched by 750 million of us worldwide: the most popular programme ever broadcast. And the nation also comes together to help *Children in Need*, when a new format, evening-long telethon in Television Centre raises one million pounds for the first time ever. And Pudsey Bear makes his first appearance this decade as the charity's enduring mascot (1985), named after the in-house designer's home town!

In the 1980s too, Frank Bough and Selina Scott launch *Breakfast Time* (1983), which moves to Television Centre five years later. Daytime television also begins in this decade (1986), amalgamated from a range of different programmes. Our daily relationship with television will change forever.

In the early evening, Wogan becomes the new Parkinson, interviewing the great, the glamorous and the good in his regular chat show. Meanwhile, Jeremy Paxman completely changes the tenor and tone of news and current affairs interviewing, challenging politicians as never before with a much tougher and more incisive line of questioning.

Keeping us laughing are the diverse scenarios of *Yes Minister*, *Hi-de-Hi!*, Rowan Atkinson in *Blackadder*, *Alas Smith and Jones*, *'Allo 'Allo*, *French and Saunders* and *Birds of a Feather*.

Only Fools and Horses launches in 1981 and becomes one of the most popular BBC comedies ever (remember the escapades of Derek 'Del Boy' Trotter, Rodney and Grandad in their unforgettable Robin Reliant car?). The series brings the little three-wheeler back in fashion, but more importantly, holds the accolade for the highest UK audience ever for a sitcom episode (the 1996 episode, 'Time on Our Hands' is watched by 24.3 million viewers!)

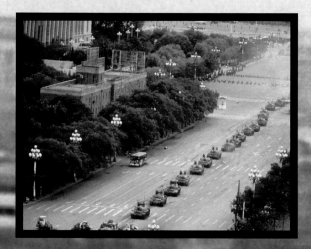

Crisis
Talks

*"The noise of gunfire rose from
all over the centre of Peking.
It was unremitting…"*

1989: BBC Foreign Correspondent Kate Adie,
Tiananmen Square, China.

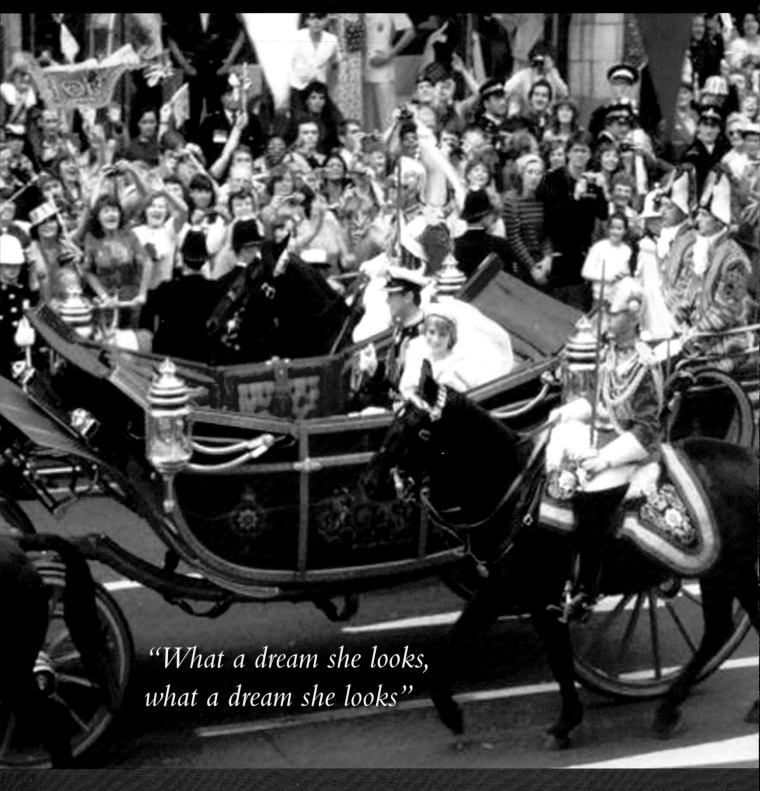

*"What a dream she looks,
what a dream she looks"*

1985: The effervescent and ever-popular Terry (now Sir Terry) Wogan has fronted countless BBC TV and radio shows. He also gave huge support to the BBC's charity appeals, and here he is (above) with Gloria Hunniford as 'Sonny & Cher' in the Children in Need spectacular.

1993: Sir Terry - then just plain 'Terry' - with the Children In Need mascot, 'Pudsey Bear'.

1985: Horrified by the starvation in Africa, Bob Geldof galvanised world leaders, the general public and fellow pop stars to raise millions for the cause.

Comedian Lenny Henry sporting his red nose for Comic Relief.

"Give us your money! Now!!"

Left:
John Stapleton and his wife Lynn Faulds Wood tracked down everyone from dodgy tradesmen to culpable captains of industry.

Right:
Sue Cook and Nick Ross in search of Britain's most wanted.

"Don't have nightmares"

WATCH IT - WATCH OUT!
Watchdog, Crimewatch and Newsnight

"Did you threaten to over-rule him?!"

Yes Minister
and Yes Prime Minister

"A career in politics is no preparation for government."

*Paul Eddington, as 'Jim Hacker', Nigel Hawthorne as
'Sir Humphrey Appleby' and Derek Fowlds as 'Bernard'. The series
became essential viewing for all of us, and residents of Westminster
and Whitehall especially. Written by Sir Antony Jay and Jonathan Lynn
and produced by Sydney Lotterby.*

It happened here...
The Lesbian Avengers

In 1988, a group of gay women (calling
themselves 'Lesbian Avengers') invaded
the 6 o'clock News studio in protest
against government anti-gay legislation.
Presenter Sue Lawley kept her cool,
while her BBC colleague Nicholas
Witchell was obliged to sit on one of
the women, as she had chained herself
to his chair!

"Balderdash Darling"

"Does it involve two pencils
up your nose Baldrick?"

Blackadder

Blackadder *featured the inspired comic writing of
Richard Curtis, Rowan Atkinson and Ben Elton, and was
produced by John Lloyd. However, perhaps the most
surprising moment was the last episode of the final
series, 'Blackadder Goes Forth'. This hugely moving
and unexpected end sequence saw the comedy cast
going over the top to face the German guns on the
Western Front during WWI. The montage ended silently
in slow motion, the soldiers dissolving into the image of
a field of poppies.*

"I have a cunning plan..."

*Back row: Tim McInnerny as 'Captain Darling',
Stephen Fry as 'General Melchett' and Hugh Laurie as 'Lieutenant George'.*

*Front: Rowan Atkinson as 'Captain Blackadder'
and Tony Robinson as 'Private Baldrick'.*

French & Saunders

The creative collaboration of Dawn French and Jennifer Saunders arguably reached its height when their final series featured lavish homages to movies and music stars past and present.

Here Bette Davis (French - left) and Joan Crawford (Saunders - below) are given the treatment in the duo's hysterical parody of the 1962 movie, 'Whatever Happened to Baby Jane?'.

"Old squishey legs"

Gordon Kaye as 'René' with Vicki Michelle as the sexy, siren waitress, 'Yvette'.

'René' with his wife 'Edith' (Carmen Silvera).

'Allo 'Allo

" *Good moaning. I admit my Fronch could be butter.*"

Arthur Bostrom as 'Captain Crabtree', the British Officer with an accent problem.

Created by Jeremy Lloyd and David Croft (*Are You Being Served?*), this delicious 'French farce' notched up 85 episodes over ten years

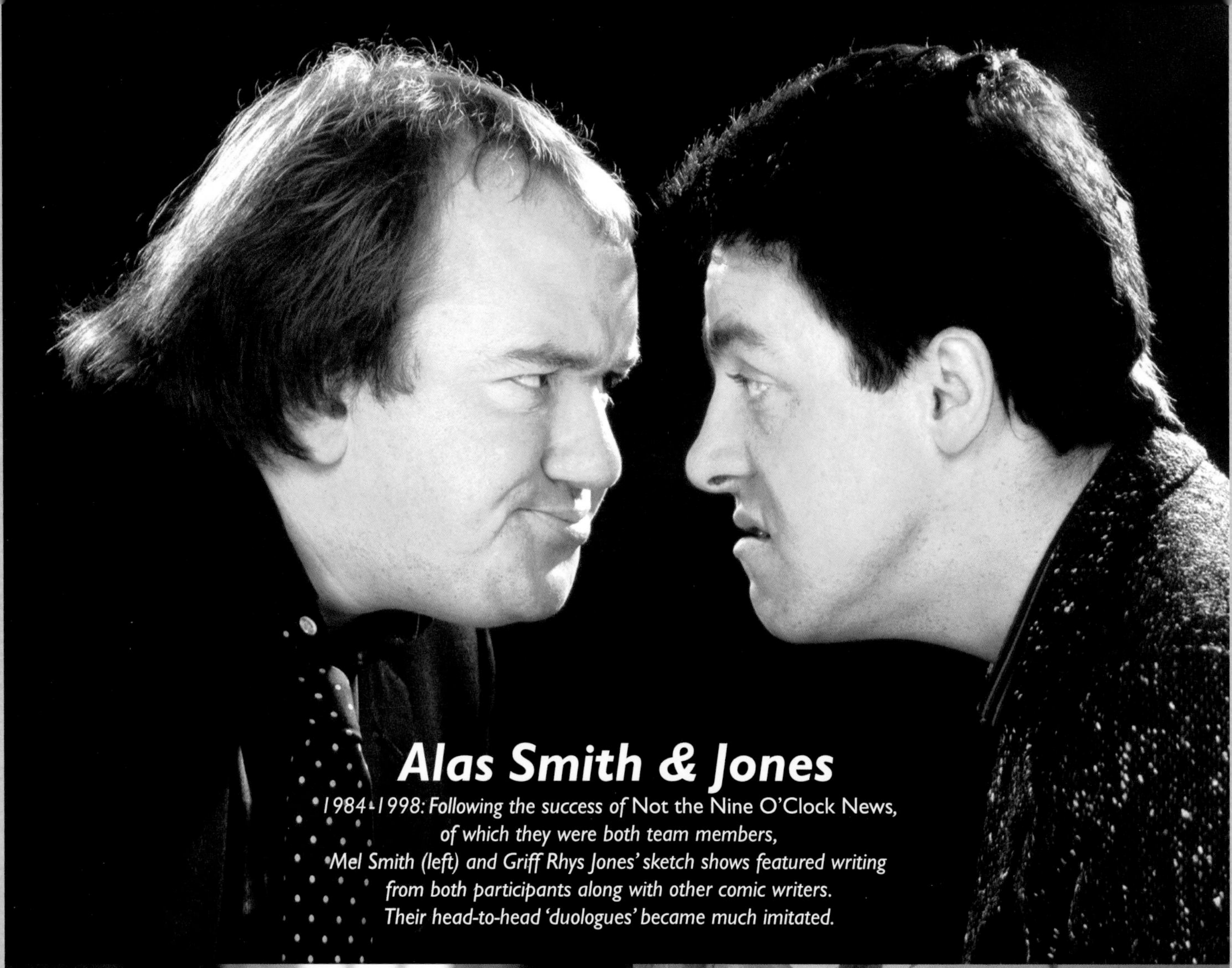

Alas Smith & Jones

1984-1998: Following the success of Not the Nine O'Clock News, *of which they were both team members, Mel Smith (left) and Griff Rhys Jones' sketch shows featured writing from both participants along with other comic writers. Their head-to-head 'duologues' became much imitated.*

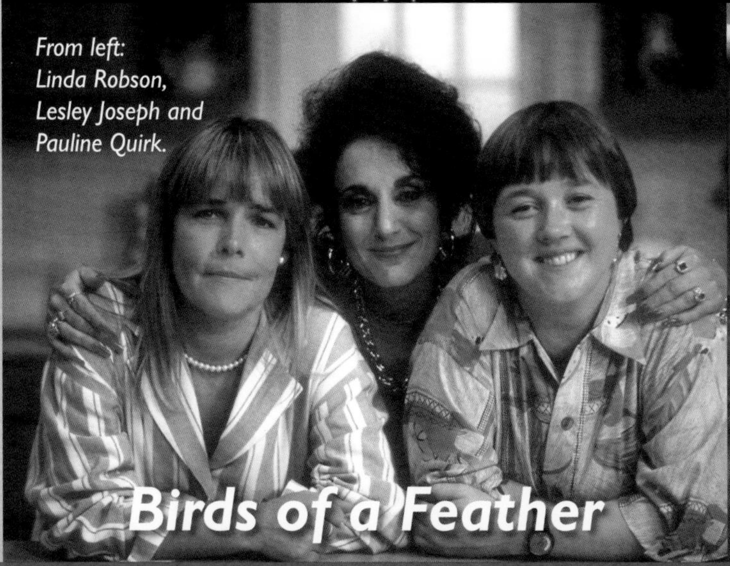

From left: Linda Robson, Lesley Joseph and Pauline Quirk.

Birds of a Feather

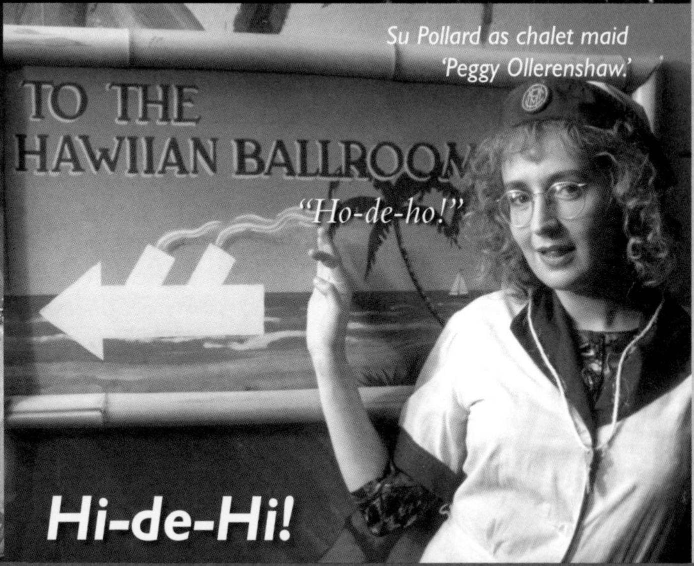
TO THE
HAWIIAN BALLROOM
"Ho-de-ho!"

Su Pollard as chalet maid 'Peggy Ollerenshaw.'

Hi-de-Hi!

Alas Smith & Jones parodies in its title the popular Western TV series of the 1970s, *Alias Smith & Jones*

"You plonker!"

Only Fools and Horses

Created by John Sullivan, this sitcom set in South London's
Peckham, starred David Jason (now Sir David), as 'Del Boy
Trotter', Nicholas Lyndhurst as his younger brother Rodney
'Rodders' and initially, Lennard Pearce as their ageing
grandfather. He was later replaced by Buster Merryfield
(he of the great beard!), as 'Uncle Albert'. The supporting
cast included Roger Lloyd Pack as 'Trigger', John Challis as
'Boycie' and other great characters. The scenario was simple:
archetypal market traders and their futile attempts to get
rich. The series, unusually, gained both popular and critical
acclaim, winning a string of major awards and accolades.
In a BBC poll of 2004 it was voted
Britain's best ever sitcom.

Their yellow three-wheeler Robin Reliant 'Regal' van achieves cult status, and sales of vintage examples rocket   55

"Ohh"

Inspired by previous TV 'greats' Peter Cook and Dudley Moore, The Pythons, Reeves and Mortimer, Paul Whitehouse becomes HUGE!

SUIT YOU SIR - the 1990s

The 1990s see big changes in how the TV industry works and how programmes are made, and this of course impacts on production at Television Centre. More and more programme making moves out of London, more of it is made by independent TV companies (as commissions for the BBC), while drama is increasingly made on location – in fact, the last large studio-based drama made in Television Centre was the stylish 1920s drama, *The House of Eliott* (1991 -94).

BBC Comedy is as ever alive and well, producing a string of popular, studio-based hits – who could forget Edina and Patsy with all their bad habits in *Absolutely Fabulous*? Or the notoriously grumbling persona of Victor Meldrew (*One Foot in the Grave*), the ridiculous social snobberies of Hyacinth Bucket (pronounced 'Bouquet' please!) in the aptly named *Keeping Up Appearances* – not forgetting the wonderful comic creations of *I'm Alan Partridge*, Victoria Wood's *Dinnerladies*, Judi Dench and Geoffrey Palmer's delicate sparring in *As Time Goes By*, and of course the myriad characters from *The Fast Show* with its new comedy mantra: get the character on, get them to say something funny, get them off?!

This is also the decade when we have lottery fever – the creation of the National Lottery and its transmission live at the heart of the weekend schedule have us all back in our living room armchairs on Saturday evening glued to those revolving balls. And no-one here at Television Centre will ever forget the momentous draw in November 1996 when the draw machine failed to start…

BBC Sport maintains its flagship series *Grandstand* and *Match of the Day* at the Centre in this period, and launches the hugely popular sports quiz, *They Think It's All Over* in 1995, fronted initially by comedian Nick Hancock and sports personalities Gary Lineker and David Gower.

For children, *Live and Kicking* brings fresh entertainment formats to Saturday mornings – launching the careers of Andi Peters, Emma Forbes, Zöe Ball and Jamie Theakston, among others. At its peak, over 2.5 million children tuned in. For adults, entertainment finds a home in Crinkley Bottom – remember that? – where Noel Edmonds has his *House Party* (1992), catching celebrities on camera ('Gotcha!') and creating the ubiquitous Mr Blobby who goes on to have his own TV show as well as a hit record!

Colin "Lord spare us from office jokers" Hunt.

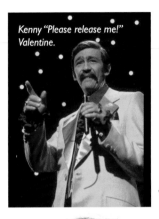
Kenny "Please release me!" Valentine.

"It's Brilliant!"

Poula "Scorchio!" Fisch, weather woman.

Duke "With my reputation" of Wymbourne, the 13th.

"I wouldn't know about that Sir"

Charlie Higson and Paul Whitehouse

Dinnerladies

'Dolly'
Thelma Barlow

'Jean'
Anne Reid

'Brenda'
Victoria Wood

'Anita'
Shobna Gulati

'Twinkle'
Maxine Peake

"We're out of 'Bollie', darling!"

Absolutely Fabulous

1992-1996 and 2001-2004: Joanna Lumley as 'Patsy' (left) and Jennifer Saunders, who also wrote the series, as 'Eddy'. The cast also included Julia Sawalha as Eddy's daughter 'Saffy', June Whitfield as 'Mrs June', and Jane Horrocks popped up in various guises.

Anyone who was anyone just HAD to appear in the series - as themselves:

Sylvia Anderson
Christopher Biggins
Helena Bonham Carter
Crispin Bonham Carter
Jo Brand
Fern Britton
Emma Bunton
Naomi Campbell
Terence Conran
Daniela Denby-Ashe
Marcella Detroit
Sacha Distel
Minnie Driver
Adrian Edmondson
Britt Ekland
Idris Elba
Marianne Faithfull
Dawn French
Mariella Frostrup
Stephen Gately
Jean-Paul Gaultier
Whoopi Goldberg
Richard E Grant
Germaine Greer
Miranda Hart
Debbie Harry
Tom Hollander
Sir Elton John
Christian Lacroix
Nathan Lane
Leigh Lawson
Robert Lindsay
Lulu
Suzy Menkes
Laurie Metcalf
Graham Norton
Erin O'Connor
Bruce Oldfield
Kate O'Mara
Anita Pallenberg
Suzi Quatro
Zandra Rhodes
Mandy Rice-Davies
Richard and Judy
Miranda Richardson
Kristin Scott Thomas
Meera Syal
Twiggy
Rufus Wainwright
Ruby Wax
Dale Winton
Clarissa Dickson Wright

One Foot in the Grave

Keeping Up Appearances

1990-2000: One Foot in the Grave, *by David Renwick, ran for six series spanning the decade. Richard Wilson played the terminally irritable 'Victor Meldrew', Annette Crosbie his resigned wife.*

1992-2005: Co-writer of The Good Life, *Bob Larbey created* As Time Goes By, *an intelligent sitcom of middle-aged star-crossed lovers, played with great charm by Geoffrey Palmer and Judi Dench.*

1990-1995: Keeping Up Appearances, *created by Roy Clarke, starred Patricia Routledge as the snobbish, provincial, Hyacinth Bucket (pronounced 'bouquet'), and Clive Swift as her hen-pecked husband.*

1991-1994: The House of Eliott: *Stella Gonet and and Louise Lombard starred as sisters in Jean Marsh and Eileen Atkins' 1920s couture saga.*

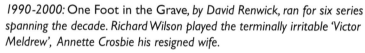

As Time Goes By

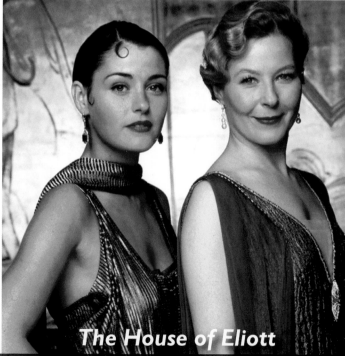

The House of Eliott

Noel's House Party (with Mr Blobby)

Noel Edmonds' House Party on Saturday evenings proved very popular, with his celebrity 'gotchas!' being the highlight. Here (above left), Noel - inside 'Mr Blobby' - surprises GMTV's Lizzie Roberts. Mr Blobby was 'invented' by Noel Edmonds himself.

The National Lottery Live

It happened here...
Spice World 1997

Meeting extra-terrestrials and spending a night in a haunted castle were not enough for the The Spice Girls in their 1997 movie *Spice World*. Their adventure was only made complete by a visit to Television Centre, home of *Top of The Pops*. Other films which used Television Centre as a scenic backdrop include *Iris* and *Atonement*.

The National Lottery Live has enjoyed a number of presenters. Among them Anthea Turner and Gordon Kennedy, and more recently Dale Winton.

Later with...Tony Bennett.

Later with... Johnny Cash.

Later with... K D Lang.

Later... with Jools Holland

began in 1992 and has been running ever since, attracting an eclectic range of solo performers, live bands, ensembles - from Paul McCartney to Kate Nash and Alicia Keys, from Oasis and Radiohead to Gorillaz. Jools Holland really loves Television Centre, and the style of his show has always reflected that, especially the opening 'jam' sessions with Jools at the piano inviting all his guest artists to improvise along with him.

STRICTLY BRITAIN - the 2000s

The big shift in this decade is the increasing use of the studios at Television Centre by broadcasters other than the BBC. This comes about because of the creation of BBC Resources (now called BBC Studios & Post Production), a new commercial divison of the BBC responsible for marketing BBC services to the wider media industry. So visitors to the Centre are often surprised to see C4 and ITV productions being made here – including recently *The Alan Titchmarsh Show*, *The British Soap Awards*, *The Charlotte Church Show, Harry Hill's TV Burp* (all for ITV); *Boys & Girls, Without Prejudice, The New Paul O'Grady Show* (all for C4).

But big BBC entertainment shows still pour out of Television Centre – notably the hugely popular *Strictly Come Dancing*, fronted by Bruce ('Nice to see you, to see you NICE!') Forsyth and Tess Daly, which drives the whole country (world!) dance-crazy. Plus Graham Norton and Andrew Lloyd Webber turn us all musical-obsessed, with the talent shows *How Do You Solve a Problem Like Maria?*, *Any Dream Will Do* and *I'd do Anything*, all creating new stars of stage and small screen. *Top of the Pops* also continues here until its demise in 2006, while *Later...with Jools Holland* gives us quality late-night music across the styles and genres.

Comedy is never in short supply from Television Centre. *The Catherine Tate Show* introduces us to a parade of memorable characters (who can forget the provocative Lauren – 'face? bovvered?' – who flummoxes even Tony Blair), as does the taboo-smashing *Little Britain*, from Daffyd ('the only gay in the village') to Emily Howard and Florence ('two ladeees') and stroppy Vicky Pollard ('yeah but, no but'). There's also the inspired social satire of *Dead Ringers*, the surreal world of *That Mitchell and Webb Look*, and the twenty-somethings' humour of *Two Pints of Lager and a Packet of Crisps*.

The mantle of chat show supremo passes to Jonathan Ross in the 2000s, with his hugely popular Friday night show: edgy humour and revealing moments with guests as diverse as Ricky Gervais and Barbara Streisand. Quiz shows prove unfailingly popular, from the topical riffs and jibes of *Mock the Week* to the sporting (and not so sporting) tactics of the opposing teams of *A Question of Sport*.

Not forgetting younger viewers, for whom Television Centre never ceases to transform itself: they are invited to meet *Dick & Dom in Da Bungalow,* while perennial favourites such as Basil Brush and the tantalising tales of *Jackanory* reinvent themselves for each generation.

Bruce Forsyth's television debut was in 1939 and he has entertained ever since. Aged 76, he begins hosting 'Strictly'

"Face? Bovvered?"

The Catherine Tate Show

There was no escaping the larger than life characters of The Catherine Tate Show *and* Little Britain *in the 2000s - in-your-face and provocative, with memorable catch-phrases that became short hand for recognisable social types almost overnight. So just imagine if Lauren met Vicky Pollard met Daffyd met Emily Howard and Florence…?!!*

Meanwhile, in another part of Television Centre, Connie Fisher (left), was winning the star West End role of Maria in How Do You Solve a Problem Like Maria?, *presented here by one of this decade's most popular personalities, Graham Norton - salacious chat show host turned family-friendly presenter.*

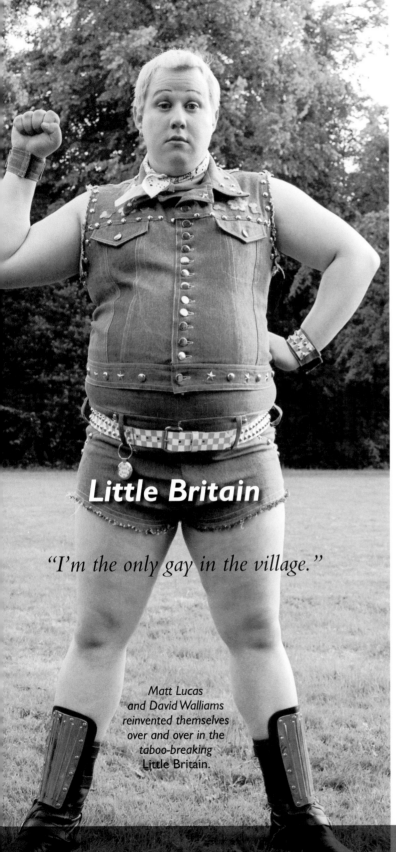

Little Britain

"I'm the only gay in the village."

Matt Lucas
and David Walliams
reinvented themselves
over and over in the
taboo-breaking
Little Britain.

2008: That Mitchell and Webb Look -
cock and bull stories.

It happened here...
Alan Johnston 2007

June 2007: colleagues of BBC Gaza
correspondent Alan Johnston at the Television
Centre newsroom, and at BBC offices around the
world, observed a vigil to mark 100 days since his
kidnapping. The newsroom went quiet at 1315
GMT, the time Alan Johnston had been abducted.

2003: Some children's programmes just run and run: Basil's new look for CBBC, with 'Dave' - Stephen Hayes, 'Stephen' - Chris Pizzey and 'Molly' - Georgina Leonidas.

"Boom-boom!"

The Basil Brush Show

1963: Magician David Nixon (see page 5) gave Basil his big break when he appeared on The Nixon Line. Five years later in 1968 the lovable fox was given his own show - The Basil Brush Show.

For twelve years Basil and his 'real-life' stooges - initially 'Mr Rodney' (Rodney Bewes of The Likely Lads fame) gave a whole generation of children a warm and wonderful pre-bedtime treat on Saturdays. In 2002 Basil made a comeback and in 2003 appeared in several Friday episodes of Blue Peter, as a presenter.

"HA HA HA!:" Television Centre provides a hiding place for Britain's favourite fox.

Playschool *on set.*

Homework: Phil Redmond's Grange Hill.

Dick & Dom in Da Bungalow.

Johnny Ball, Carol Leader and Derek Griffiths in Playschool.

Jimmy Savile in Jim'll Fix It.

John Sessions in Jackanory.

John Craven and his perennial Newsround.

'STRICTLY'

The energetic Angelica Bell.

FOR KIDS!

Phillip Schofield and sidekick 'Gordon the Gopher'.

Jamie Theakston and Zöe Ball: the stars of Live and Kicking.

Children's favourites across the years, from *Playschool* to *Grange Hill*, from *Live and Kicking* to the perennial *Jackanory* and *Newsround*

Strictly Come Dancing

1959: Come Dancing's judging panel, a very sober affair all round in the late 50s.

2008: The winner takes it all! Holby City actor, Tom Chambers, seen here with dance partner Camilla Dallerup, holds the glitter ball trophy aloft.

2008: BBC Political Correspondent, John Sergeant (fourth from left) with dance partner, Kristina Rihanoff. Despite his lack of dance skills, the public votes kept him in week after week. His voluntary departure from the show prompted national headlines.

2007: Singer Alesha Dixon and her dancing partner, Matthew Cutler tripping the light fantastic, to win the competition that year. In 2009 she herself became a judge on 'Strictly'.

Full marks: (left to right)
Judges: Brunio Tonioli, Arlene Phillips,
Len Goodman and Craig Revel Horwood.

2004: Jill Halfpenny, with dance partner
Darren Bennett, champions with the jive.

2004: former BBC newsreader, Natasha Kaplinsky
and her dance partner Brendan Cole,
the first Strictly winners.

BBC Breakfast's
Sport Correspondent,
Chris Hollins and his dance
partner Ola Jordan were
popular winners in 2009.

Time after time, Strictly celebrities state that being on the show has been 'the experience of a lifetime!'

BBC

Want to know more...?

Tours

Of course absolutely the best way to find out more about Television Centre is to go on a tour, where you get an exclusive look into the BBC Newsroom, see the famous studios, and venture into the dressing rooms and green rooms that have hosted so many famous guests over the decades.

And as well as Television Centre, did you know that there are over 20 more BBC buildings you can visit too? These include the iconic home of BBC Radio, Broadcasting House in London, The Mailbox in Birmingham where *The Archers* is recorded, Scotland's brand new broadcast centre at Pacific Quay on the banks of the Clyde, and the other national centres in Cardiff and Belfast, as well as many local BBC stations.

For a complete list, visit: bbc.co.uk/showsandtours

Audience shows

Why not take in a show while you're visiting too? From *Strictly Come Dancing* to *Later... with Jools Holland*, from *The News Quiz*

to a live BBC concert, there are thousands of audience tickets available – and they're absolutely free! Go to: bbc.co.uk/showsandtours

History

If you fancy finding out more about the history of BBC broadcasting – how radio and TV began, a timeline of broadcasting innovations, weekly anniversaries and objects in our BBC Collection – then simply log on to: bbc.co.uk/historyofthebbc
There's lots more to discover, each and every week.

The BBC in general

And for information about the wider BBC – what's on air, making comments and suggestions about our programming, getting a job with us, BBC organisation and structure – go to the comprehensive BBC website: bbc.co.uk

1960 **BBC** 2010
TELEVISION CENTRE

Design and editorial by Nick McCann.
Decade introductions by Robert Seatter, Head of BBC History.
Front and back cover montage by Nigel Gibson.
Heritage House Group Publishing Director, Paul Torjussen.

Many people helped in the development and production of this publication. With especial thanks to the following: Dick Fiddy and Marcus Prince at the British Film Institute; BBC colleagues in the Photo Library, News Stills Library, Written Archives, History teams for invaluable research and support; Ralph Montagu at Radio Times; Ollie Burton and Andy Begg, BBC Audience Services.

Produced and published by Heritage House Group, Ketteringham Hall, Wymondham, Norfolk NR18 9RS www.hhgroup.co.uk
All photographs are BBC copyright except pages 20, 24 and 35 (main pictures) which are copyright Getty Images. Design copyright Heritage House Media Ltd. Whilst every effort has been made to trace the owners of copyright material reproduced

ISBN 978-0-85101-481-4

Printed in the United Kingdom by The Burlington Press, Cambridge
91906-06/10